贝贝熊系列丛书
The Berenstain Bears'

学会理财
DOLLARS AND SENSE

AF807910

孩子们喜欢有自己的钱——他们自己手里的一元一分。但是，钱是该花掉还是该存起来——怎样理财才有意义呢？

第一时间的启蒙书

1
1
PAPA
SISTER

贝贝熊系列丛书

The Berenstain Bears'

学会理财

DOLLARS AND SENSE

（美）斯坦·博丹　简·博丹　绘著

Stan & Jan Berenstain

孙志芳等　译

父母和孩子一起阅读

家长和子女共同成长

新疆青少年出版社

在通往熊王国深处的一条金色土路旁，有一座大树屋，树屋里住着贝贝熊一家。对他们来说，钱不是什么大问题。但钱又是个问题——至少小熊兄妹很关心。他们对钱已经多少有些了解：他们知道爸爸不是用钱做的，钱也不是从树上长出来的，而且要存一些钱来应付糟糕的日子。这些事情熊爸爸已经告诉过他们好多次了。他们不清楚的，是应该怎么安排自己的钱。

小熊兄妹很喜欢钱，甚至在他们还不知道钱能用来买东西之前就喜欢上了。比起纸币来，他们更喜欢硬币，因为硬币有很多种玩法。

他们喜欢在地上滚着玩；

他们喜欢在桌子上转着玩；

他们喜欢把硬币摞起来玩；

等又长大了一点儿，他们喜欢玩“正面还是背面”的游戏。

但是在超市、工具店、服装店……他们睁大了眼睛观察一切，仔细听着每一句话，很快就明白了钱还有更多的用处——除了能用来玩，还可以用来买东西。

一共9美元20美分。

一共11美元10美分。

钱可以买到各种各样的东西——

从“快乐熊”那里买冰激凌；

在商场玩跳跳鸭；

从公园里卖气球的叔叔那里买气球。

渐渐地，小熊兄妹学到了更多关于钱的知识。他们知道了美元和美分符号的区别：美元是“S”，中间有两条竖线；美分是“C”，中间有一条竖线。

虽然他们还是很喜欢硬币，但他们也知道了用纸币可以买到更多的东西。

“棒球卡？婚纱？”熊爸爸嚷了起来，“你们一定觉得我是用钱做的吧！你们一定觉得钱是从树上长出来的吧！”孩子们都缩了回去。他们想要的只不过是一点儿绿色的纸币，得到的却是爸爸的红脸。

熊妈妈一直在旁边看着。她知道是时候该把事情平息一下了，而且她已经想好了一个办法。

“如果你们不介意，”她对小熊兄妹说，“我有点儿事情要跟你们爸爸商量。”

“亲爱的，”熊妈妈说，“对孩子们大呼小叫没有任何好处。他们不清楚钱是怎么一回事，也有我们的责任。我们应该教会他们怎样理财。”

“那要怎么教呢？”熊爸爸问。

“我建议从现在开始每周给他们固定的零花钱。”熊妈妈说。

“嗯，”熊爸爸说，“这个主意不错。没准儿他们能学会该怎么花钱呢。”

"零花钱？"小熊妹妹说。

"零花钱是什么？"小熊哥哥问。

"零花钱就是，"熊爸爸说，"在每个星期的第一天，你们会得到一小笔钱。由你们自己决定要怎么安排它们——是存起来还是花掉，你们觉得怎么合适就怎么办。"

001

姓名

地址

日期

支付形式 $

美元

不可背书转让

熊王国银行

用于

记录

日期

零花钱

支出

零花钱剩余

001

002

姓名

地址

日期

支付形式 $

美元

不可背书转让

熊王国银行

用于

记录

日期

零花钱

支出

零花钱剩余

002

003

姓名

地址

日期

支付形式 $

美元

不可背书转让

熊王国银行

用于

记录

日期

零花钱

支出

零花钱剩余

003

记录

日期 ______

零花钱 ______

支出 ______

零花钱剩余 ______

004

004

姓名 ______

地址 ______

日期 ______

支付形式 ______ $ ______

______ 美元

熊王国银行

用于 ______ ______

不可背书转让

记录

日期 ______

零花钱 ______

支出 ______

零花钱剩余 ______

005

005

姓名 ______

地址 ______

日期 ______

支付形式 ______ $ ______

______ 美元

熊王国银行

用于 ______ ______

不可背书转让

记录

日期 ______

零花钱 ______

支出 ______

零花钱剩余 ______

006

006

姓名 ______

地址 ______

日期 ______

支付形式 ______ $ ______

______ 美元

熊王国银行

用于 ______ ______

不可背书转让

孩子们互相看了一眼，好像不相信爸爸说的话一样。因为这件事情太棒了，棒得有点儿不像是真的。

“这是你们第一个星期的零花钱。”熊爸爸说。

小熊哥哥和小熊妹妹看着熊爸爸放在他们每人面前的一小叠钱。然后他们抓起钱，冲出大门，下了台阶，往镇上跑去，快得你还来不及告诉他们：“这是一周的零花钱。”

“有问题。”熊爸爸说。
“大有问题。”熊妈妈说。

当小熊兄妹回来时，他们一人捧着一把棒棒糖、一把泡泡糖，还有各种卡片。

在这个星期的第一天，他们就花光了所有的零花钱。

下一周他们干了同样的事情。

再下一周又是这样。

再下一周还是。

对熊妈妈和熊爸爸来说，零花钱这个主意不像预想的那么有效，而且很明显，根本没有教会孩子们怎么用钱。

很快，小熊兄妹就会把所有的棒棒糖都吃掉，对买来的其他东西也都失去了兴趣。然后他们开始不停地抱怨，因为在这个星期剩下的几天里，他们一分钱也没有了。

“妈妈，”小熊哥哥说，“我觉得这个零花钱的主意根本不管用。”

“我非常同意，”熊妈妈说，“那么你有什么建议？”
“更多的零花钱！”兄妹俩异口同声地回答。
“也许吧，”熊妈妈说，“但这件事得跟你们的爸爸商量。”
“那我们现在就去找他商量吧！”小熊妹妹急切地说。

“哦，这可不行，”熊妈妈说，“爸爸正在写支票簿。我从不在这个时候打扰他。”

“嗯，支票簿，”熊妈妈心想，“我和熊爸爸就是用支票簿来理财的。这能让我们有机会想想这些钱该怎么花，而且能记录下来我们已经花了多少，还剩多少。”

熊妈妈进了厨房，她在橱柜的抽屉里仔细翻找了一下。抽屉里装满了她舍不得扔掉的东西。其中有几本多余的支票簿，是她换银行时留下的。但是该怎么向孩子们解释支票和支票簿的用法呢？

熊妈妈把她的想法告诉了熊爸爸。然后，她把用支票的主意向孩子们解释了一下。

“你是说，要把我们的零花钱拿走吗？”小熊哥哥抗议道。

“当然不是，”熊爸爸说，“实际上，我们要给你们更多的零花钱。但是我们会替你们保管，而不是在一周刚开始就把钱给你们，要不然你们还没等它在口袋里捂热就全花光了。这样，当你们需要点儿零花钱，或者想要买点儿什么东西的时候，就写张支票出来。”

“来，我给你们示范一下。”

“首先，你先写上‘现金’，就像这样。然后写上你要花多少钱——既要写上数字也要写上大写，这样就不会出错了。接着，在这行写上这笔钱用来干什么，在最底下这行和背面签上名。然后把它交给妈妈，她就会把钱给你们，并保管你们留下的存根。就这么简单。”

小熊哥哥马上就有了主意，他给了妈妈一张三美元的支票，熊妈妈立刻就给了他现金。他本来想花五美元（零花钱的一半）买棒球卡，但是他改变了主意，换成了一本棒球书。小熊妹妹也改变了主意。她决定把第一周的零花钱省下来，用下一周的零花钱去买芭比熊的婚纱，这样她还能剩下十美元。

“这样，才是我说的理财啊。”熊妈妈满意地对熊爸爸说。

The Berenstain Bears'

DOLLARS AND SENSE

Cubs like their own money—their own dollars and cents.
But to spend it or save it—what makes the most sense?

1. Money wasn't a big problem in the Bear family's tree house down a sunny dirt road deep in Bear Country. But it *was* a problem—at least where cubs Brother and Sister were concerned. They knew some things about money. They knew that Papa wasn't made of it, that it didn't grow on trees, and that they should save it for a rainy day. Papa had told them those things many times. What they didn't know about money was how to manage it.

2. The cubs liked money. They had liked it even before they knew you could buy things with it. They liked coins better than paper money because you could do things with coins.

They liked to roll them.

They liked to spin them.

They liked to stack them.

As they got a little older, they liked to play "heads or tails" with them.

3. But by keeping their eyes and ears open at the supermarket, the hardware store, and the clothing store, they soon learned that you could do a lot more with money than just play with it. You could *buy* things with it.

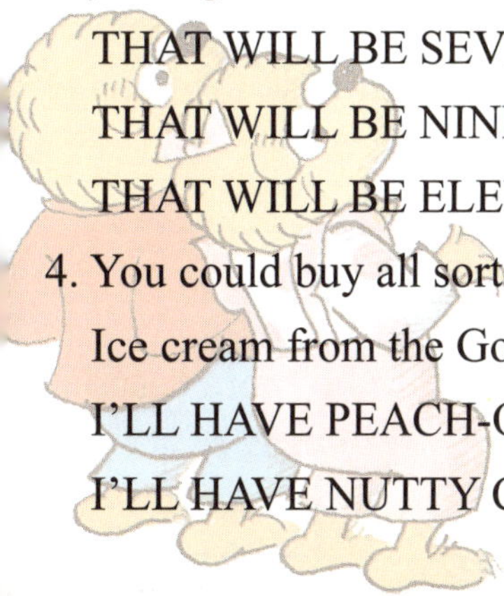

THAT WILL BE SEVEN DOLLARS AND FIFTY CENTS.

THAT WILL BE NINE DOLLARS AND TWENTY CENTS.

THAT WILL BE ELEVEN DOLLARS AND TEN CENTS.

4. You could buy all sorts of things.

Ice cream from the Good Humor Bear,

I'LL HAVE PEACH-ORANGE WITH JIMMIES.

I'LL HAVE NUTTY CHOCOLATE CHERRY.

rides on the Bucking Duck at the mall,

HI-OH, DUCK !

balloons from the balloon bear at the park.

I'LL HAVE RED.

I'LL HAVE BLUE.

5. As time went on, the cubs learned more about money. They learned the difference between the dollar sign, which was an "S" with two lines through it, and the cent sign, which was a "C" with one line through it.

And while they were still fond of coins, they learned that you could buy a lot more with dollars.

PAPA , MAY I HAVE FIVE DOLLARS? BASEBALL BOB IS HAVING A BIG BASEBALL CARD SALE.

PAPA, MAY I HAVE TEN DOLLARS? MY BEARBIE DOLL IS GETTING MARRIED AND SHE NEEDS A WEDDING DRESS.

6."Baseball cards? Wedding dress?" shouted Papa. "You must think I'm made of money. You must think money grows on trees!" The cubs backed away. All they wanted was some green money. All they got was Papa red in the face.

Mama had been watching. She knew it was time to calm things down, and she had an idea how to do it.

"If you cubs will excuse us," she said, "there are some things I'd like to discuss with your papa."

7. "My dear," said Mama, "it's not going to do any good to shout at the cubs. It's as much our fault as it is theirs that they don't understand about money. It's up to us to teach them how to manage money."

"But *how*?" asked Papa.

"I suggest that we begin giving them a regular weekly allowance," she said.

"Hmm," said Papa. "That's an interesting idea. Then perhaps they will learn to be more responsible about money."

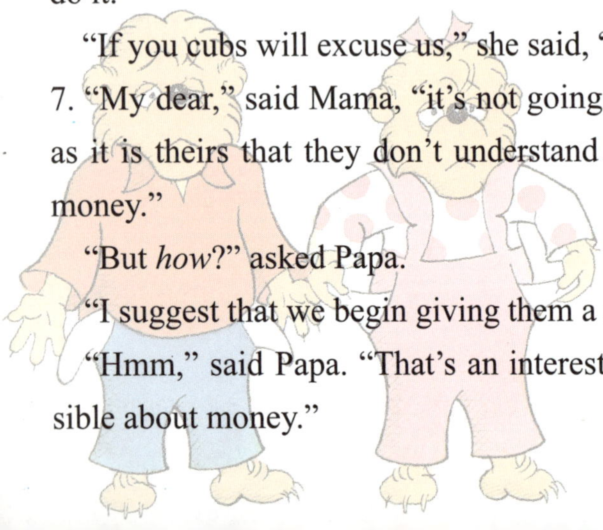

8. “An allowance?” said Sister.

“What’s an allowance?” asked Brother.

“An allowance,” said Papa, “is a sum of money that you will get at the beginning of every week. It will be up to you to manage it—to spend it or save it as you see fit.”

The cubs looked at each other as if they didn’t believe him. It seemed too good to be true.

9. “And here’s your first week’s allowance,” said Papa.

Brother and Sister looked at the small pile of money Papa had placed in front of each of them. Then they grabbed the money and were out the front door, down the front steps, and on the road to town faster than you can say “weekly allowance.”

“Hmm,” said Papa.

“Double hmm,” said Mama.

10. When the cubs returned, they each had a pile of candy bars, bubble gum, and trading cards.

They had spent their whole allowance on the first day of the week.

And they did the same thing the next week, and the next, and the next.

11. It was clear to Mama and Papa that the allowance idea wasn’t working as planned, and it certainly wasn’t teaching the cubs how to manage money.

The cubs would quickly eat the candy bars and get tired of the other things they bought. Then they would mope and groan because they didn’t have any money left for the rest of the week.

“Mama,” said Brother. “I don’t think this allowance idea is working out.”

“I quite agree,” said Mama. “But what do you suggest?”

“*A bigger allowance!*” said the cubs as one.

“Possibly,” said Mama. “But that is something we’ll have to discuss with your papa.”

“Well, let’s discuss it with him right now,” said Sister.

“Oh, no,” said Mama. “Papa is balancing the checkbook. I never interrupt your papa while he’s balancing the checkbook.”

12. Hmm. Checkbook, thought Mama. Our checkbook helps Papa and me manage *our* money. It

gives us a chance to think about how we should spend it. It gives us a record of how much money we have spent and how much we have left.

Mama went into the kitchen. She rummaged around in the cupboard drawer. It was filled with things she wasn't quite ready to throw away. Among the things were some extra checkbooks that were left over from when she changed banks. But how to explain the idea of checks and checkbooks to the cubs, she wondered.

13. Mama told Papa what she had in mind. Then she explained the idea of checks to the cubs.

"Do you mean you're taking *away* our allowances?" protested Brother.

"Not at all," said Papa. "As a matter of fact, we're increasing your allowances. But instead of giving them to you at the beginning of each week so that you can go out and spend them before they burn a hole in your pockets, we're going to hold them for you. Then when you want a little pocket money or want to buy something, you write out a check.

14. "Here, I'll show you how it's done.

"First you make it out to 'Cash,' like so. Then you put how much it's for—in words as well as numbers so there can't be any mistake. Then you write what it's for on this line and sign it at the bottom and on the back. Then you give it to Mama and she gives you the money and keeps a record. It's that simple."

Brother got the idea right away and gave Mama the check for three dollars, and she gave him the cash. He changed his mind about spending five dollars (half his allowance) on baseball cards and bought a baseball book instead. Sister changed her mind, too. She decided to save her first week's allowance and buy the Bearbie wedding dress with her *next* week's allowance so she would still have ten dollars left.

15. "Now, that's what I call *money managing,*" said Mama to Papa.

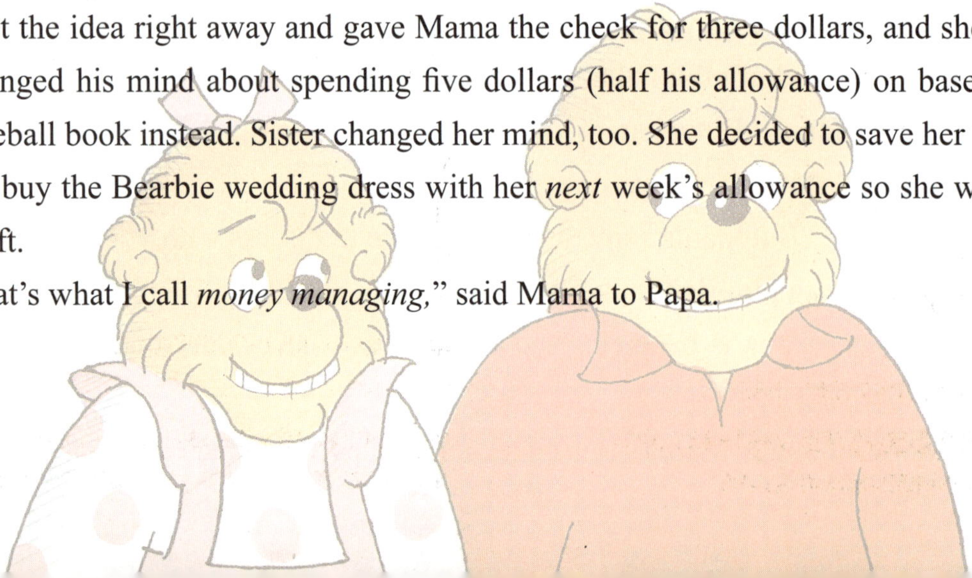